PRAISE FOR ARE YOU A MAGDALENE?

My life often includes moments of profound "AHA" and a deep feeling that something is happening beyond me, beyond my control, and will often lead me to tears. Reading *Are you a Magdalene?* created one of those moments and answered my prayers. Being touched on a soul level has become something I embrace and ask for daily.

Feeling recognition within my soul while reading a book only keeps my attention more. I experienced moments of such recognition and shed tears I believe were triggered simply from remembering. If you are on any kind of soul-searching mission, trying to find meaning or simply wanting to see life, our souls, and our history in a completely new way, this book is a must read.

Understanding that I do not know much has opened opportunities to learn about subjects and discover history that has proved to heal me, open my mind, help me forgive and most importantly feel and know my soul.

This book is now part of that process in my journey of life, and I am grateful to have had the opportunity to read it. Truly loved reading this book. Sat and read it today in one sitting. You completely got my attention. And of course, you made me cry.....AGAIN!

~ Salvatore Candeloro, Medium by Design

Are You a Magdalene?

Discovering Your Divine Feminine Heritage and Purpose

Are You a Magdalene?

Discovering Your Divine Feminine Heritage and Purpose

CATHERINE ANN CLEMETT

Second Edition

ISBN: 978–0–9847209–3– 4

DEDICATION

I dedicate this book to all the Magdalenes past, present, and future who have seeded the light for eons who now are here to blossom and harvest that light into the brilliance of the new earth.

CONTENTS

ACKNOWLEDGMENTS

I wish to thank Anna (the grandmother of Jesus), Claire Heartsong, the Hosts of Heaven, the Magdalenes, the Holy Family, and all of those light beings on the other side of the veil assisting us with our ascension. I also wish to thank all who have attended my workshops, tours, and events for you have all contributed your wisdom, your light, and your dedication to fulfilling the Magdalenes' mission.

Chapter 1—Is Your Soul Calling You?

Your soul is calling you to remember your heritage and purpose, for the timer has now gone off. Probably, what drew you to this book is your interest, fascination, or hunger for knowing more about Mary Magdalene. As you probably are aware, there are many portrayals of Mary Magdalene.

Mary Magdalene, customarily portrayed in the Catholic Church and elsewhere as a sinner and prostitute, is actually the archetypal representation of the stigma of being born a woman, representing the oppression and repression of women which has gone on for centuries. Many believe her to be the wife of Jesus.

There is much speculation whether this is true, whether they had children, and what this all means.

Other accounts portray Mary Magdalene as a follower of Jesus, one of his core group members, who witnessed his crucifixion and burial. Believed to be the first one to witness his resurrection, some have referred to her as the Apostle to the Apostles. The greater truth about Mary Magdalene is that she was an adept and a profound teacher equal to Jesus. There is now a resurgence of interest in Mary Magdalene surfacing with a proliferation of books coming out as well as a new controversial movie. This is because of the awakening happening en masse on the planet now.

Mary Magdalene reminds us, not only did Jesus have a partner and a mate in his life, but it is time to heal the imbalance of the masculine and feminine in our world. It is now the time for the return of the Divine Feminine to take its rightful place of equal honor, power and authority next to the Divine Masculine. Mary Magdalene has always been a teacher and example of this. There is, however, a much larger picture at play here.

As you read this book, I ask you to feel into it with your heart. For this is not information readily available through research, theological texts or investigations. For some of you, it will be a very unconventional perspective, even controversial. If the information resonates with you, embrace it. If it does not resonate with you, you are not only free, but encouraged, to let it go. Accept only that which resonates within your being or sparks the possibility of a new way of thinking.

Although sometimes this information may challenge your belief systems, you will intuitively know if there is 'truth' in it for you. Although your mind may not understand it and it may not fit the ideas and constructs offered you through religious teachings you may have received, it might spark some distant memory, or feeling deep within you which you didn't even know was there.

It is best to approach this material through your heart more than your mind. Allow the unfolding and flowering of the wisdom to occur there. Allow yourself to be fully present. Enjoy the story. If possible, reserve your judgment until you have finished reading the entire account.

Chapter 2—Magdalene Is an Order of Consciousness

In 2006, I came to understand the name Magdalene didn't refer to just the individual, Mary Magdalene, but represented a much larger overseeing group consciousness. Many beings have been part of the Magdalene Order throughout many lifetimes, including this current lifetime. I share this information because many of you may be Magdalenes who are being asked by your souls to remember who you are.

When you know that there is a Magdalene consciousness coming forth now, it may help you have a greater understanding of certain feelings you've had or patterns which exist in your life. This understanding may also help you have the courage and confidence to explore rather than dismiss what you know deep down and to not be afraid to access your soul's memory, even though these are not necessarily things you may know in your conscious mind at this point.

Just having the awareness and the support of the Magdalenes may help you delve into your soul memory so you can step forward because you may have awareness, wisdom or information to share which is needed now.

This understanding may also help you get beyond any doubts or thoughts of "Who am I to do this?" Or maybe you have a tendency to hold yourself back simply because you don't think you have the authority or credibility to put yourself out there and take a risk. This is also because you may not remember who you are.

Chapter 3—Who Are They and Why Are They Here?

The Magdalenes, as a group consciousness, has existed not only since the beginning of the planet but even before the creation of Mother Earth. They have been present in every age and every culture on the planet under many diverse names and labels.

The feminine aspect of the Magdalenes in ancient Egyptian times went by the name The Daughters of Isis. The Magdalenes have shown me they are part of an interdimensional race whose purpose is to 'seed the light'. They bring the light into the deepest, darkest places so that the light will not go out, often where no one else will go.

Do you know that expression 'where angels fear to tread'? Usually, this saying has an interpretation of being a fool; it refers to someone who, out of ignorance, goes into a difficult or dangerous situation because they don't know any better. This could also apply to Magdalenes however in a different way. Those who are Magdalenes even though they may have no conscious awareness that they are Magdalenes, may often find themselves in challenging or difficult situations, not because of their ignorance, but because of their innocence and vibrational ability to hold the light although this ability may not be conscious.

Whenever there is a shift of consciousness, or a planet, or system which is ascending, there is a massive incarnation of Magdalenes into that system as volunteers. The Magdalenes refer to themselves being the 'midwives' of the shift of consciousness. Deep within their souls, within their innate cosmic beingness, they have the gifts, tools and intrinsic know-how to assist in the resurrection and ascension processes that the planet and its inhabitants are going through. Even though the human mind of the incarnated Magdalenes (many of you) may not consciously know this, the understanding continues to unfold and comes forth as needed.

Have you ever had the experience of sharing some information, healing, energy or perspective that you didn't know you knew? You may have had a feeling of it being incredulous or perplexing to you as you wondered where that awareness, or thought, came from.

Maybe you resonate with the information about Mary Magdalene because she was, and is, a profound being and a spiritual teacher equal to Jesus. Jesus or Yeshua (his name in his native Aramaic language) could not have accomplished what he did without his twin-flame essence of Mary Magdalene. Nor could he have accomplished what he did without the support of the other Magdalenes and Essene community members, for they all synergistically worked together and supported each other.

Many people find themselves enamored with Mary Magdalene because it is their only reference point for connecting with something larger they may unconsciously feel within, but don't understand. They think it is all about the individual, Mary Magdalene, when they have no awareness that the term Magdalene also represents a larger Order of Consciousness to which they may also have involvement. Focusing on the life and teachings of Mary Magdalene often acts as the catalyst for the beginning of remembrance and awareness of being part of the Magdalene Order.

For some, connecting with Mary Magdalene may trigger a deeper sense or remembrance on a soul level of being trained for lifetimes in temples of the initiates. Much of this recorded training occurred in ancient Egypt in the temples of Isis and in many other cultures and times.

This awareness of Magdalene being an Order of Consciousness can be the beginning of accessing one's soul memory. As this soul memory is activated, walking the path of an initiate, of being a Magdalene, can be not only remembered, but can be brought forward and continued in this present lifetime.

Chapter 4—Collaboration with Claire Heartsong

My introduction to the understanding that Magdalene is not only an individual but an order of consciousness came about through my collaboration with Claire Heartsong. Claire channeled the book Anna, Grandmother of Jesus, which was published in 2002. In 2006, the Councils of Light, the Master St. Germain, and Anna, put me together with Claire Heartsong as her business manager and spiritual partner.

This was after a long synchronistic series of events in

my life which took place over a twenty-five-year period engineered by the Councils of Light, on the other side, to get us together. I share the full story of this synchronistic series of events in my book, *Soulweaving, Return to the Heart of the Mother*.

Claire's book, *Anna, Grandmother of Jesus*, came about

because in the late 1980s, while Claire was in a meditation, she witnessed this large being of light standing before her. This being informed her she was Anna, Jesus' grandmother and the Virgin Mary's mother.

Some of you may know Anna as St. Anne in the Catholic Church. She went on, saying to Claire, "No one knows my story. Will you write my story?" Claire's response was, "I don't think you want me—I got D's in English. I am not the right person". Anna let her know she was indeed the right person. Over the next ten years, the Councils of Light from the higher realms worked with Claire's consciousness. By the end of this time, the Councils had finally prepared Claire to receive the downloads from Anna. If you are not familiar with the term download, it is the ability to receive spiritual information or insight from higher realms.

ST. ANNE AND YOUNG MARY, JERUSALEM, ISRAEL

This information usually carries a higher vibration or

expanded wisdom, which is out of one's usual realm of thinking or experience.

People can receive downloads either as a conscious channel, meaning their conscious mind and awareness are still present, or as a trance channel where there is no recollection of the information received. Being able to access this information is through tuning into a specific frequency, like tuning into a radio or TV station. After being prepared for the ten years since Anna had appeared to her, Claire was then ready and willing to be the conscious channel for Anna.

In the other type of channeling, trance channeling or full body channeling, the vehicle (person's body) goes into a deep sleep state where they vacate their body. This provides the opportunity for a higher level being to inhabit the vehicle's body speaking and moving through it. In this way, higher wisdom, information and energy come forth without having to go through the filters and biased thinking of the vehicle's, or channel's, conscious mind.

Examples of well-known trance channels are Edgar Cayce, Jane Roberts who channeled the Seth material, JZ Knight who channels the entity, Ramtha (in the movie What the Bleep Do We Know), Lee Carroll who channels the entity Kryon, and Esther Hicks who channels the group consciousness known as Abraham. These are but a few of the more well-known trance channels.

Whether information comes through conscious or

trance channeled sources, it is always imperative for you to discern whether what you hear, feel, or see feels right to you. Just because an entity, or being, is coming through someone, it doesn't mean they are always offering the highest, most beneficial, enlightened information.

Using discernment in determining whether your response or reaction may be a product of conditioned religious training or entrenched belief systems, or something that is responding and in resonance with your heart, will help you know if the information is valuable to you.

Sometimes experiencing channeled information is an opportunity which your soul has presented to you to expand your awareness, perspective and understanding to help you grow spiritually. Beings from the 'other side' are not that different from living humans. There are extraordinarily high enlightened beings of light with profound wisdom, healing and insight as well dark lower frequency beings who may look for an opportunity to mess with you and your energy who do not have your, or other people's best interests or highest good in mind. This does not mean you have to be fearful of this channeling process. It is just to know that you need to exercise discernment and not blindly accept everything a channel is saying just because they are a channel.

Just as people in your life may try to take advantage of you or act like energy vampires, who drain your energy or want all of your attention, not all beings on the other side are supporting your highest good. We all know people like that. It is to use your same process of discernment, trusting your gut-level feelings in all forms of interaction and communication with beings from beyond the 'veil' just like you would with humans you meet in your everyday life.

Some of you reading this may come from a more fundamentalist background and indoctrination where you're been told channeling or anything metaphysical is the devil's playground. This is not the place to go into that discussion, however, this is where again, approach this material with your own discernment, keeping an open heart and open mind reserving any judgment until the end.

MT. SHASTA, CALIFORNIA

In 1998, Claire moved to Mt. Shasta, California, knowing it was time to make herself available for receiving the download information from Anna. It took ten months for Claire to receive this information about Anna's story and type it out. However, it apparently read like a textbook. The author and publisher, Virginia

Essene, who was a friend of Claire's, started helping her with the manuscript.

She sent Claire back to square-one repeatedly to rewrite the material several times during the next three years. Finally, Virginia Essene published the manuscript, written in a novel format in the first-person voice of Anna, through her publishing company, S.E.E. Publishing in 2002.

In this book, *Anna, Grandmother of Jesus*, Anna shares the remarkable story of her life, which spanned over seven hundred years. Through her dedication to self-mastery and the arduous initiations she underwent, she brought forth a spiritual lineage that changed the world.

In this book Anna also shares the conditions which eventually led to her birthing the cast of characters who brought forth not only Jesus, but many other characters involved in the Christ drama. Anna could do this because she was one of a handful of initiates who'd learned to survive physically the arduous ancient Egyptian Rites of the Sepulcher.

Many did not survive these initiations. Those trained in these rites, who successfully mastered them, could maintain physical immortality in the body indefinitely as long as they kept periodically doing these rites. Claire Heartsong shared all of this material in the first Anna, Grandmother of Jesus book.

Claire knew at some point there was to be a sequel to the first book, which continues on with what happened to the Holy Family and the Essenes after Jesus's crucifixion, resurrection and ascension.

Knowing that there was to be a second book, Claire had a bit of a tantrum with the Councils of Light, saying she did not want to be shut away like a little monk working on the second book by herself. She demanded they send her a support team. This is how my friend CW and I arrived at Claire's doorstep in 2006 as her support team.

My friend CW and I moved from Portland, Oregon to Springdale, Utah, which is the town at the entrance to Zion National Park. Claire had moved there a few years earlier. This was the perfect place to bring forth this work, as it was in the twelfth dimensional vortex field of the Great White Throne, one of the mountain peaks in Zion National Park.

After three weeks of getting settled, working on Claire's website, networking our computers together, and attending to all the other business details, we were finally ready as Claire's support team so she could start channeling the information for the second book. The next day, Claire was ready to start the sequel to her original book Anna, Grandmother of Jesus. She went to the computer in her bedroom to channel the information for the sequel

After two days of writing, she emerged from her bedroom frustrated and dejected.

Claire addressed Anna, "I can't seem to get into the same heightened energy which I experienced when receiving the download from you for the first book. What is the problem?"

Anna, "The answer lies outside the door. Go ask

Catherine Ann for a regression session. (One of my healing modalities is doing past life regression sessions with clients.) The Councils of Light have a somewhat different plan in mind for the second book, which includes your threefold energy."

THEO, CLAIRE'S CAT, ANCHORS ENERGY

I lay Claire down on the living room couch and set up a microphone and tape recorder so we could record all the sessions. Theo, Claire's Maine coon cat, had the opportunity now to do his job. During the session, he would climb up on Claire's body either laying on her heart or her legs, to help anchor the energy coming in during these sessions.

Initially, I used the induction protocols from my training in past-life regression with the author, Dolores Cannon. Soon Anna and the Councils of Light came in and gave us a very specific process and protocol to use specifically for these sessions in which information from nineteen distinct characters came through. This information eventually became the framework for the second book, Anna, the Voice of the Magdalenes.

It amazed Claire how much easier this process was than sitting alone at her computer, typing away. During this time spent with Claire channeling Anna, Anna introduced many groups of people to the understanding about Magdalene being an Order of Consciousness.

I witnessed many people interacting with Anna and how Anna helped them to understand who they were Magdalenes and how much the world needs their gifts. I believe this is relevant for many of us as well.

Chapter 5—What Does This Have to Do with Mary Magdalene?

You may wonder how all of this relates to Mary Magdalene. The narrative of the first book, Anna, Grandmother of Jesus was in the first-person voice of Anna, sharing her story as a novel.

Part of the plan for the second book was to have exchanges of nineteen distinct characters, each bringing forth their personal stories and experiences through their own 'Magdalene' voice, so the information was not solely through Anna's voice and point of view.

What came forth were many details about the daily life of the Essene community which Jesus (Yeshua) and the Holy Family were members of, along with more detailed information regarding their initiations, rituals, and even hidden information regarding Yeshua's early life. Information also came forward about what happened to the Holy Family members and the Essenes after they migrated to the south of France and eventually went to England after the crucifixion and resurrection of Jesus.

It was through facilitating these sessions and the work with Anna that we came to know the deeper understanding of Magdalene being an Order of Consciousness. Anna shared that Yeshua (Jesus) was also a Magdalene along with many other Essene women and men in their community.

The Magdalene Order includes both women and men, not just women, however the teachings of the Magdalene Order are more aligned with what we would know as the Divine Feminine teachings. We came to understand that we were Magdalenes as well.

Anna told us we had all been rehearsing for eons on the inner planes for the roles we were to step into today similar to what the characters in the first Anna book had done to prepare for their individual roles in the upcoming Christ drama of their time.

There is a chapter in the first Anna, Grandmother of Jesus book, in which all the initiates and Essenes, close to Yeshua, would go to Egypt to train in the pyramid of Giza. They would have initiations in the King's chamber because it contained a zero Point energy field crucial to their training. There, in rehearsing for the roles they were to step into in the coming Christ drama and crucifixion, they would know what their particular roles and tasks were going to be and how all of it was going to unfold. Rehearsing in the Great Pyramid would help them with their confidence with physically stepping into this drama with less fear.

THE GREAT PYRAMID

Anna informed us that, similarly, we have been rehearsing on the inner planes the roles we are stepping into today. She said that the whole Christ drama of two thousand years ago never was meant to be the focal point. It was just the 'dress rehearsal' for us stepping into our roles today.

Now Anna did not mean just the three of us, but was referring to all the awakening beings, all of those who are Magdalenes, light workers, and those on a spiritual path or who desire to make a difference. Many of these beings may not even consciously be on a spiritual path, but they try to live life from their heart, from their compassion and from a place of love.

We came to understand that there are tens of thousands, if not millions, of what Anna terms, Magdalenes, alive on the planet today. We also knew that many of us, who particularly feel a close alignment with Yeshua, the Christ drama and those times two thousand years ago, are the future selves of those Essenes, members of the Holy Family, the disciples and Yeshua's followers. Working with the Magdalene consciousness, the Magdalene energy has taught me to not get hung up on labels.

Many who are Magdalenes will never know consciously who they are. They would not identify with being labeled as a Magdalene. They may never know the effects of what they do, yet they are still rehearsing their roles on the inner planes.

For a more in-depth understanding of what it meant to be a Magdalene in Anna's time, I am sharing an excerpt from the book, *Anna, the Voice of the Magdalenes* by Claire Heartsong and myself. In this session, Claire and I exchanged roles. I instructed Clare how to facilitate the session. In this excerpt, Lizbett, the character I brought forth during a session when Claire regressed me, responded to questions from Claire about a coming-of-age initiation she experienced where she shares her understanding of what it means to be a Magdalene.

"CLAIRE: How old are you, Lizbett?

LIZBETT: I am thirteen. I will be fourteen in two more months. Some of the girls are twelve. The oldest is sixteen. Some of the girls in our village have children at our age, but we are on a different path. It is not that we are not allowed to have children at some point later in life; it is just that we are choosing a different training or path of teaching.

We young girls, who are coming into our womanhood, are being taught how to carry the information and the codes to a different fruition. We are taught how important it is to be able to utilize our wombs for a higher energetic exchange and a higher alignment with our mates. Whether we do this for our enlightenment or for allowing a greater divinity to come forth when we have our children, it is done with much more loving awareness.

CLAIRE: Did your mother and daddy bring you into the world in this way?

LIZBETT: Oh yes. It was a very sacred exchange, a blessed moment, sanctioned by all the Councils of Light.

CLAIRE: Why do you suppose your mother is called Magdalene?

LIZBETT: She is of that family and that spiritual lineage.

CLAIRE: Does that make you a Magdalene now?

LIZBETT: Yes. Not a fully initiated Magdalene, but a Magdalene at the first level of training.

CLAIRE: Please tell me what your understanding is about being a Magdalene.

LIZBETT: I carry the genetics and the potential for being a Magdalene, which are carried from generation to generation. But just having the Magdalene genetic codes does not make me a Magdalene.

There has to be a willingness and readiness of mind, body, and soul. To walk as a Magdalene requires much study, contemplation, and cleansing of thoughts and emotions. There are activations or transmissions of spiritual energy that must come down and awaken the codes that are held in the earth's elements of the body. Then there can be an ignition of a spiritual fire within. When this happens, it ignites internal pathways of knowledge to be expressed in external paths of service. Then you can be addressed as a Magdalene.

Some Magdalenes have to look back many generations to find their genetic connection. To be a Magdalene is not by birthright alone. It is through a deep desire and a willingness to be trained and taught. It is accomplished in collaboration within a lineage of those who have gone ahead of you. It is an honoring of those who walk with you, and it is an honoring of your own physical and emotional self.

When all the required elements are present, there is the uniting of the memory and the ancient wisdom that is carried through lifetimes into the present incarnated self. Then one holds the mantle and the staff of the Magdalene. It is a great honor to never be taken for granted. A Magdalene vows to never bring harm or to feel superior or prideful.

CLAIRE: Are there men who are Magdalenes, or is it only women?

LIZBETT: There are men aligned in a similar order. They are the protectors or knights of the Magdalene. They receive their own similar experience of teaching and fusing higher dimensions of divinity into awakening the codes held within physicality. The frequencies are a little different for the men whose path of service brings together the union of spirit and flesh, but they go about it with a slightly different focus than the women.

It is important to understand that the codes may be carried in a female body in one lifetime and then in a male body in the next. The soul has the opportunity to experience a full spectrum of how the Great Mother, through her Magdalene sons and daughters, helps all living beings return to her full embrace. Some of the Druids carry this ancient wisdom and they work in harmony with those of us who are called Essene-Magdalenes.

On certain occasions of teaching and ritual, the men and women come together. Because there is a slightly different complementary frequency and function, the initiated men and women can come together like a lock and key in a powerful fusion. This is needed for conceiving more awake children in the Light, for conscious dying and rebirth, for the Rites of the Sepulcher, and other things that we do not share with those who would not understand.

CLAIRE: Do you need a partner to have these fusion experiences?

LIZBETT: No. You can do it all by yourself. But it is very helpful to learn in increments with a partner. The partners may change with time, as either one may develop faster than the other, or one may be better suited for a particular ritual and not the other. My parents (Yeshua and Mary of Bethany) and sister (Sar'h) and other relatives were my first partners, like when my mother and I circulated energy with each other. There may be a series of partners, both men and women, until we are ready to be with our partner who perfectly meets our highest destiny.

Then there is a perfect fusion and a perfect fit on all levels. Then we can create an incredible energetic field. There is an energetic interpenetration like a pulse that goes out and then it returns, amplifying and magnifying the joined partners as they join with the Light of the Beloved on High (as Grandmother Nana calls the unnamable God). It is like the sacred triangle. The two people are the base of the triangle and the Beloved is the point at the top, where they both join. They are equally joined at every point of the triangle.

Then the triangle becomes a powerful generator of energy like the Great Pyramid in Egypt where my parents took some of their Magdalene initiations. Information and wisdom is gathered and experienced. There is a spiraling out and in of greater and greater magnitudes and more and more dimensions."

Chapter 6—The Magdalene Mission

Around 1986, all of my friends were on a spiritual path. Many of them were fellow students of Ramtha channeled by JZ Knight. It amazed me that all of us had suffered abuse of some sort. We all suffered either mental, emotional, physical, or sexual abuse. I questioned at the time how come all of us who were on a spiritual path had suffered such abuse.

The conventional 'spiritual' answer at the time was that it was karma. We had all suffered abuse because of 'bad' things we did in other lifetimes. We were paying the penalty for those 'bad' things now. Occasionally, this is true for people, but I just knew that was not the case.

It was not correct. In meditation, I asked my guides to give me the correct answer. I didn't get it right away, but a few weeks later received this 'download'.

Inner Guidance: "You are not a victim. You are a volunteer. It is because of your spiritual strength and fortitude that you have entered this situation of suffering emotional abuse through being born into your dysfunctional family. If you can make it through, without your Spirit being broken, you will begin to dissolve the mastermind programming that exists there, freeing yourself and helping others to become free as well."

This answer, I felt, was the truth. It was the precursor for my understanding who the Magdalenes were, and are, when they came into my conscious awareness some twenty years later. This was the definition of who a Magdalene was. They are the ones who volunteer (often unconsciously) to go into the deepest darkest places where no one else will go because they are carrying out their mission of 'Seeding the Light'.

In traveling the world and sharing this understanding in workshops, talks and Grid Activations, I have met many Magdalenes who, just by having this perspective, have a better understanding of who they are. Many who are Magdalenes have often felt like they are victims or that they are weak. They can't seem to rise above their circumstances. Some of them may even give up, numbing themselves with drugs or alcohol, going into depression, succumbing to other forms of mental illness, or feeling hopeless, defeated and unworthy. Some of them are even so challenged by their lives and circumstances, not understanding who they are; they can't take it anymore and end up committing suicide. It is all because they have forgotten who they are and that they volunteered to 'seed the light' in the deepest, darkest places where no one else will go.

They may find themselves in dysfunctional families, jobs, corrupt institutions, corporations, business and the like wondering why they are in those situations, particularly if they are on a spiritual path. They may wonder what they did wrong to deserve where they are. They are often looking for the light, the person or the situation that will rescue them and pull them up out of it. They don't realize that being a Magdalene they are the light for everybody else.

They are like the lighthouse providing the light in the darkest of places and situations often giving hope to those around them. Just by having this understanding, the shift of perspective of being a Magdalene and remembering who they are, can change the scenario immensely. Of course, this may not be the case for all Magdalenes, but many I have encountered have felt this way.

Magdalenes are here now to help restore the rightful place of the Divine Feminine on earth. It is the Divine

Feminine consciousness connected to the 'Great Mother' who births all reality from the womb of consciousness, knowing all life, all form and all dimensions are a holographic interconnected web of life where every particle and every atom of life and form contains the blueprint and the wisdom of the whole. This is the memory that the Magdalenes are being called upon to re-introduce to planet earth now.

The Divine Feminine has been repressed, suppressed and defiled for so many millennia now that a great imbalance has occurred on planet earth affecting her people, her resources, her elements and her very stability. This balance must be restored for the planet and all of us to survive and thrive.

This is why the Magdalenes have volunteered to return to planet earth now, for we have the wisdom, the codes of light and the tools, deep within our souls to remedy this situation. Remember the purpose and heritage of the Magdalenes has always been to 'seed the light' and introduce higher vibrational frequencies to planets and systems that are awakening and ascending.

As the old paradigm of patriarchal domination continues to shatter and disintegrate, we Magdalenes have come forth now in this shift of consciousness to help re-establish the emergence of the Divine Feminine once again out of the shadows so that the Divine Feminine and Divine Masculine can come together in Divine union or unity consciousness upon the planet.

Chapter 7—Meeting Other Magdalenes

Magdalene's are present in all places, in all cultures, in every country, in all religions, organizations, institutions and professions. In my travels around the globe giving workshops and awakening Magdalene Divine Feminine grid lines in different locations across the planet, I have met several extraordinary Magdalenes, both women and men. It is like we Magdalenes carry a certain resonance. On a subconscious level, we recognize each other.

It is not uncommon for people who carry the Magdalene energy to feel they don't fit in. I know I have felt this for most of my life. As I've encountered other Magdalenes in my travels, this was not an uncommon feeling shared by many of them. Meeting other Magdalenes is like having a deep soul connection.

It is like finding one's 'tribe'. Anna (the grandmother of Jesus) refers to this 'tribe' as 'the family' meaning the family of the light, the Christed energy. She is not referring to family being the literal lineage or bloodline, but to those that embody a state of consciousness which allows for unity, which facilitates the upliftment of all life. The 'family' comprises those beings who live from their hearts and strive to live unity consciousness personified, embodied, right here, right now.

These Magdalenes, or 'family' as Anna refers to us, have scattered throughout the planet often found in the most unlikely of places; in politics, corrupt institutions and organizations, in professions or jobs that you wouldn't consider spiritual. They are across the board from the most spiritual places and endeavors to the densest and seemingly unenlightened places and jobs. Remember that the Magdalenes 'volunteer' (usually before being born into this life) to go into the deepest darkest places to 'seed the light'.

Two of the most profound interactions with Magdalenes, in unlikely places, for me were both with Muslim men. The first one was our bus driver on a tour to the south of France in 2006, led by Finbarr Ross. Before meeting our bus driver in France, he had confided in Finbarr how terrified he was about driving Americans. Never having met Americans before, he thought we were going to hate him because he was a Muslim, as this was a few years after the attack on the

World Trade Center in New York City on 9/11.

When I met him, I felt an immediately felt a strong bond of soul recognition and love. He was truly a Magdalene male. We all felt close to him. It didn't matter that he was a Muslim man living in Toulouse, France. True to the countenance and mission of the Magdalene male, he was very protective of us, always looking out for us. Concerned about our welfare, he never hesitated to go above and beyond his duties to assist us and make things easier for us.

While visiting the Cathar sites in the South of France, when we climbed down to the sites below, he would walk along the upper rim at the top, just making sure we were all okay. When the tour was winding up and we no longer needed the bus and his services, we said goodbye to him. It was a very emotional parting, as there was such a bond of love and familiarity. I will never forget him.

The other Magdalene male, whom we had a profound experience with, was also a Muslim. I facilitated a Magdalene Grid Activation in Ephesus, Turkey where I needed to hire a van and the driver of the group. I asked to have an English-speaking driver to make things easier. Assured he spoke English however, even though I was told he spoke English, he spoke no English. As he was driving, I often caught him glancing back at the group through his rear-view mirror. I am sure our group was an enigma to him, not like other American tourists he'd encountered at his job. We were not typical Americans. Of course, he didn't understand what we were saying.

The first out of the ordinary event with him came when we were at Pamukkale, a most remarkable place in Turkey with terraced lime stone pools. This turned out to be one of my all-time favorite places which I have experienced during my travels. Also, at Pamukkale are hot spring pools which have existed for thousands of years. It is said the Holy Family and the Essenes these same hot springs two thousand years ago. These were very unusual hot springs in that the hot spring water covers an entire area of submerged ancient ruins. Because the water was very deep and clear, we could see we were easily swimming over what look like Grecian columns and other architectural ruins on the bottom of the springs. It was quite a unique experience.

PAMUKKALE LIMESTONE POOLS

To enter these hot springs cost an additional fee which we paid. We were surprised when a little while after we entered the hot springs, our Muslim driver paid his own way and came into the pool to join us.

This was unusual for him to elect to take part in an activity with us. Towards the end of our tour, we came together to do the actual ceremony and ritual for the Grid Activation, which our group had been preparing for throughout the entire tour. In the ritual of activating the grid, we came together in unison, in a unified field. We acted like a human acupuncture needle for this spot on the planet.

We accomplished the activation of this planetary point through meditating, toning, ingesting elixirs, applying sacred oils to our chakra points, movement and other things considered "woo-woo" to those people who do not understand the use of these things as tools to raise the frequency of our group in creating a unified field.

I initially planned to do this ritual for the Ephesus, Turkey Magdalene Grid Activation at the site of the Virgin Mary's house in Selcuk, Turkey. However, as a major tourist attraction, the Virgin Mary's house was too heavily fenced and guarded along with too many tourists for us to do this type of ceremony publicly.

We found a place about eight kilometers away, on a beach, on the Aegean Sea. We walked down the beach to find a spot to do our ceremony. Our driver lagged behind not quite sure what he should do. He motioned to us, gesturing to us if it was okay if he joined us. I thought to myself, okay, what can I do? He is our driver. I motioned to him to join the circle. When he did, I was absolutely amazed how fully he took part in everything we did with us.

Even though he didn't speak English, or understand what was being said, he just followed everything the rest of us did including allowing himself to be anointed with oils, ingesting certain elixirs, lying down on the sand in geometric patterns and basically doing whatever we were doing, without hesitation. When it was all over, we returned to the hotel. He walked up to one of the front desk personnel, asking them to translate for him. He put his arms around the two men in the group.

The first thing he said, which he asked the front desk personnel to translate was "These are my brothers! These are my brothers!" Then he asked through the translator, "What did you do to me? My heart will never be the same." He had had a profound experience even though he didn't understand the language. It became clear he was indeed a Magdalene who felt called to be part of this Grid Activation, and evidently, he also had rehearsed with us on the inner planes. It was an extraordinary experience and sharing for all of us.

There is much to rediscover, uncover, and remember about the Magdalenes and their history upon the planet, as well as how Magdalene may relate to you. In the time of Anna, Yeshua and the Essenes, they were all trained as high tantric masters. They were masters of alchemy often evolving to the point where they were in control of their environment and the elements.

At various times I have asked my guidance, from the higher realms, to share information regarding the Magdalenes with me. Below is a compilation of some of these 'downloads'. Even though Magdalenes are both women and men, the Magdalenes particularly are involved with bringing the Divine Feminine back into balance and into its rightful position.

When the Divine Feminine returns to its rightful place, then the masculine aspect rather than expressing as the 'out of balance' patriarchy, can emerge as the true Divine Masculine who honors and protects the Divine Feminine. When the Divine Feminine and the Divine Masculine are equal, in balance and both honored and revered equally once again, twin flame union ensues, bringing everything back into unity consciousness, or Oneness, once more.

This is not about only the reunification on the human level but the ending of all separation where there is no longer a need for suffering or duality any more. This is what the Magdalenes have always been working towards.

Chapter 8—The Magdalene Ascension Codes

As Magdalenes, we carry within us certain dormant frequencies. Our intent can activate these frequencies when we honor them and have a willingness to become more conscious of our energies carried through our thoughts, words, and actions. Upon doing this, we can more easily connected with the light frequencies instilled by Yeshua, the Essenes, and the Magdalenes into the elements, the genetic lines, and the earth plane for this time of ascension.

These teachings powerfully seeded within us now are calling forth to be remembered as we've been the ones called forth to serve humanity and the planet through this shift of the ages.

Inner Guidance from Anna and the Magdalenes:

"We are so happy and so pleased that you are opening yourself and dedicating yourself to this project for it is a worthy endeavor whose time has come. The time of ripeness is at hand. The codes of the Magdalene Order are ancient teachings, configurations and ways of being passed down, orally and energetically, mostly through rituals and initiations from mother to daughter and through the sisterhood of souls known as the Magdalenes—the female Christ initiates. For it is they who hold the balance of power of the Divine Feminine— the Mother of Creation and of matter into form and form into matter, for it is a paradox. It is like a Celtic knot.

Allow yourself the privilege of communing with nature, with the elements, for all are present within you and around you at all times; the very ground upon which you exist— where you walk, obtain sustenance and dwell; the very air that you breathe and the gentle breezes that caress you. And of course, there is the life-sustaining water that you ingest that hydrates form and the ground; the fire element —the sun that ever gives forth of itself for light and life on the planet, which reflects in the moon and the fire, the light reflected in the twinkle of the stars. It is these elements; these forms of nature, when in balance, are the great nurturing and sustenance of your plane and your being.

However, when they are out of balance, these elements become great destructive forces of nature, rectifying that which is askew, rectifying that which magnifies disharmony, disconnection and that which unfolds as personal and planetary dysfunction. Now is the time of remembrance and re-member–ing, realizing everyone and everything is a member of the whole. It can be no other way. You are part of that whole as is everything and everyone.

It is the time to claim misguided, misused, misspent creations, for they all are configurations of energy, energy which you can reclaim and remold such as when you use modeling clay. The whole is your temple; the temple of your body and the temple that is your planet. How are you treating these temples? You as Magdalenes know how to resurrect and reform this misguided energy, thought forms and creations. This is part of the training you've received as initiates. Find the peace and the balance of the elements and forces within you, so that they will eventually reflect in the elements which surround you, bringing peace and sustenance once again.

In your world, it appears there are many voices. There isn't one voice which is more important than the others, there is only the Oneness speaking through many facets.

There is much chaos in your world pulling you in many directions.

Call upon the wisdom and the energy in the strength of all, within the lineage, within the line. This is what it means to be of a certain lineage, to be of what we could term the Magdalene lineage. Indeed, for you then are able to access that inner energy, wisdom, innovation, creativeness, and all that has gone before, or will come after you, in shaping and bringing forth what is most pertinent in the moment to be shared.

Allow yourselves to become finely tuned, to tune into that frequency which brings forth that which is most appropriate and most needed, in any individual moment. This will not only affect you; but through you, will reach out to many and awaken many, for they will fiercely feel things they have not felt before. They'll start becoming aware of things in a more personal way, in a different way.
They will come into alignment within their

own beings and will no longer be only a talking head. Many have not known that there was even another experience other than being a 'talking brain.' They'll find they have feelings which may be uncomfortable for they don't understand what is happening and what they should do with them.

The discomfort will only be momentary as they discover who they are and that they are multifaceted beings with much they can own in themselves. They will discover they are more than their human self, more than their perceived small self.

You, as a Magdalene, will 'seed the light' and indeed be a catalyst for deeper exploration for many. You all will have opportunities to be of 'service' to humanity, to the whole. This is what you have rehearsed on the inner planes for eons, to come into fruition now. Some of you will be active as teachers, healers, channels, inventors, bringers of the new technologies, new systems and new ways of being as the planet shifts into the New Earth. Others of you may be the ones who pray, who go within, doing the deep inner work to hold and anchor the light for many.

Even though you may do this quietly in the background, thinking you aren't doing anything, never-the-less it is an important contribution, for you, as a Magdalene, will be an example showing them.

You will open worlds of knowledge and understanding not even fathomed by them before. We will help open the doors for this happening. We just wish you to understand the larger picture. It is time now to step forth in a much larger way, for there is a ripeness, an unfolding and a quest for understanding that is now needed and is ready to happen.

We have been preparing many for a long time. It is time to know that the rehearsals for this time period are now winding down. For are you not well prepared to take your places? Your mind may not know what this means, but your soul does. Know that we Magdalenes in the higher realms honor you, support you and guide you in every step.

Make a conscious decision to connect with us and ask for our help. If you prefer, you may call upon any of us, as individuals, or call upon us, as a group. You may call upon Mother Mary, Mary Magdalene, Anna, Yeshua, any of the Saints, masters, angels or other members of the Holy Family, or the Magdalene Consciousness to support and assist you.

We recognize and honor your sovereign being, your divinity, and know that you are one with us and equal to us. Call upon us!"

Chapter 9—Who are Present-Day Magdalenes?

Apresent-day Magdalene is not someone who is necessarily Christian. You do not have to believe a certain way, follow the Bible or follow a particular religious protocol or set of rules.

One of the most 'Magdalene' people I know is a sound healer who channels awesome ancient Jewish chants. She is very Jewish. Even though she lives in the United States, two of her three children live in Jerusalem, Israel, as very conservative Jews. All six of her grandchildren were born there and are being raised there. She isn't exactly comfortable telling her conservative Jewish family that she hangs out with Yeshua, Anna, and the Holy Family.

In another instance, while facilitating a workshop in southern California, this woman called me after the workshop had already started asking if she could come late to the workshop. She told me she kept receiving emails about this Magdalene workshop which I was facilitating, but figuring it was a Christian thing, would repeatedly delete them.

Finally, she had a strong feeling she needed to take heed, pay attention to it, and come to the workshop. When she arrived, she shared her story, saying she hadn't any idea what this workshop was about or why she was 'called' to be there. Besides, she said, "I am Jewish". By the end of the workshop, she absolutely knew why she was there. It was because her soul knew she was a Magdalene. It had nothing to do with her religious beliefs. Her soul had prompted her to be there.

So, what makes up a present-day Magdalene? Ultimately, it is someone who has compassion and empathy for all life and all people. It is someone who more and more, is learning to live from their heart, not their head. It is someone who honors the sanctity of all life and all paths, who sees the interconnectedness of everything. It is someone who has evolved enough in their soul journey to do their own 'inner work'.

They're willing to look inside themselves to see what trauma, faulty beliefs and issues are there that need to be cleared, or healed, rather than projecting these outward, lashing out and blaming everyone around them. It is also someone who is beginning and willing to look inside to discover that the answers lie within them. They are willing and even eager to embark upon the journey of experiencing and realizing that divinity starts within.

Know that as present-day Magdalenes you are here now because you are needed. You have a piece to share, something uniquely needed by the whole, which is contributed by you and through you. You, as a present-day Magdalene, have been an initiate in the temples for many lifetimes to prepare for your journey today.

The light is 'seeded' within you. You are here to share that light. You are not here reading this book by accident. In fact, you aren't even incarnated into human form in this lifetime by some random chance. It is all by Divine Design, designed by you and Mother/Father God. To unfold your path and awareness as a Magdalene, (you need not adopt that label) or a light worker or someone who just wants to be 'of service', it is first to willingly attune more to your intuition and inner guidance for that is your inner guidance system.

It is also to take some time each day to be grateful for all you have and your unfolding journey. It is to go within and start developing a greater relationship with your own higher self, your own 'I AM' presence and your own Councils of Light who are assisting and guiding you from within. It is also to not get hung up on labels, even the word Magdalene, for ultimately all are ONE.

Bless yourself for your willingness to receive. Be open to being guided from within and to being of greater service, and all will continue to unfold.

Whether your focus continues to be primarily on

Mary Magdalene or on the expanded understanding of the Magdalene Order, know you have been called, you are seen, and you are needed. One of the most remarkable things that Anna shared about Mary Magdalene was that during the crucifixion she was the only one among all who witnessed it, that never for one second lost the coherent field of energy she was holding knowing that Jesus was in ecstasy, free from pain and suffering.

This was what they all were taught to master in themselves and do as initiates. All the others witnessing the crucifixion, even those who had rehearsed their parts in the pyramid of Giza, at some point whether momentarily or for extended periods of time, faltered. They could not maintain their coherent high frequency in the overwhelming field of chaos, fear, rage and doubt that enveloped them during the crucifixion.

This was Yeshua's and Mary Magdalene's gift to us that no matter what, even during the most agonizing moments of the crucifixion, they showed they could maintain their coherent field of love, of being One with God. This is what we are being invited to do now, in these times.

Chapter 10—The Nature, Purpose, and Makeup of the Magdalene Order

In another channeling from the Magdalenes, I asked them about their true nature, their purpose and what makes up the Magdalene Order. This was their response to me:

"Dearest Lady,

We come, and we will take your question into council for it is a broad topic indeed. We are a vast council and conglomeration of beings, for lack of a better-defined term, who are a direct expression of God manifesting in form and density.

Our mission is to uphold the 'right use of energy' and the sanctity and sacredness of all life where ever we encounter it. We are the harbingers of peace, of deep reflection, of the connectedness of soul to soul, atom to atom, and world to world.

There are no simple words to convey the vastness and variety of our task and our legions for we are many, but yet, only 'one'. We are the alpha and the omega, the beginning and the end. We are the sum-total of all that has gone on before in your world.

We are the container, the essence of the meeting and the meshing of creator and the created. We are the fabric, the tapestry, where the creative out-thrusting of desire travels upon the figure eight, the infinity sign, and returns as the desire manifested to that or who originally sent out the desire or creative impulse. We are the 'Isness', the void, the conduit that holds and upholds the action of God taking place. We are the 'Sophia' - the keepers of the Grail and the 'tenderers' of the inner flame, the inner hearth.

We have come again more fully to this plane both incarnated in physical form as many of you and also as a multidimensional energy force to help awaken you, soothe you, and be your hand-maidens through this momentous shift of consciousness that is occurring.

For it is the energy and the magnitude of the Magdalene consciousness or the Magdalene Order as you are calling us that is anchoring, holding steadfast the vibration as it shifts, and propelling this new consciousness forward. It is quite a vast team effort on many levels, dimensions, many worlds, many types of beings all working towards this shift—this common goal and vision.

Many, many of you are doing your part as a Magdalene without even having conscious knowing of who you really are. For this, we are not only most humbly grateful, and have the utmost admiration for those of you in human form who volunteered for the 'front lines' so to speak. This couldn't have occurred without you.

Again, we could not have done this without you. We have waited millennia for you, beloved ones of the Magdalene, to come forth birthed in great numbers upon this plane so that through your desire for change for a better world, your dedication, your passion, and your willingness to endure whatever it takes, all life may now be uplifted, may be free, and may know itself as God fully realized.

We have you to thank for this and ask that you call upon us to be with you, to assist you so that your journey becomes sweet and your path rises to meet you, reflecting to you only profound love.

We are you. You are us. There is no separation.

Allow us to come into your life and assist you with those patterns and places that are still burdensome, painful, or sticky. Allow our presence and love to be felt in your life.

For again we hold the codes and the keys of sacred beingness wherever we are directed whether it is the most exalted of places, or the deepest, darkest, rankest, most vile of places, it matters not to us for we serve the 'one', the God within, that is found in all places, all beings, all dimensions, all vibrations. We are the container of miracles.

We serve the Christ/Christess, the unified God within. We are here now as emissaries of the Grail, as are you. We are here to help you find 'home' again within yourself. For like Dorothy in the Wizard of Oz, you have only to realize that through this entire journey you have never been apart from 'home'. You just forgot for a time. Now is the time of remembrance and re-design.

Again, we are here to be of service to you and the God/Goddess within you. This shift of consciousness that is well underway will reach a state of ripeness liken unto the fruit that is full of flavor, full of juice, full of the sweetness and divine force of life. And when this moment of ripeness occurs all the working towards, all the struggle, all the efforting will simply fall away.

And the new world, the new way of being, will be the fruit returned to you for you have surely earned it. We will rejoice with you. For then it will be done. All will be in full 'presence' within the center of their hologram.

All will be in 'rightful relationship' with all that is around them. And this new day that is dawning will be the beginning of a new wondrous and joyful adventure. It will be. Celebrate this vision and give thanks to the

God within you for making it so."

DA VINCI'S PAINTING SHOWING MARY MAGDALENE NEXT TO JESUS AT THE LAST SUPPER

Chapter 11—Where Do We Go from Here?

As challenging and difficult as these current times are for all of us, it is hard not to get caught up in the increasing exposure of evil forces upon the planet and the daily erosion of our rights and freedoms little-by-little.

A lot of us have grown up rather complacent in our experience and view of reality rarely questioning it until now. Most of us have never had to face standing up for our rights, preserving our way of life, or even having to fight for our lives as we have had to do in other lives and timelines.

At a pivotal point in the evolution of our planet, we

are being asked to remember who we are as Magdalenes, as Lightworkers, and as ones who've volunteered to come here in these times to make a difference.

Do we succumb to the lower frequencies of authoritarian control threatening to dominate all aspects of our bodies, lives, money, and ways of life? Are we so hypnotized into complacency and compliance that we don't even question what is really happening? It's time for us to wake up.

Now is the time for which we have been waiting for lifetimes. And the world has been waiting for us. In 2006, when Anna told us we'd all been rehearsing on the inner planes for eons for this time now it was also to remind us we've trained and attuned our beings in the mystery schools throughout the ages for the roles we are stepping into during this current shift of consciousness.

It is time we remember and rediscover who we are as Magdalenes. As Magdalenes, as part of this inter-dimensional group of consciousness, we are being reminded that our mission as Magdalenes is to seed the light in the deepest and darkest and to remember that we volunteered to incarnate on that planet to serve as the midwives of this shift of consciousness. This task now before us is being brought up into our conscious awareness.

We are to hold and disseminate the light coming through us with vision, empathy, and compassion. It is time now to pull up our big girl panties or big boy britches and not let ourselves get too distracted by the drama and chaos unfolding around us. The Hosts of

Heaven and Councils of Light have channeled the message below to help us better understand our place in these times.

We are the Midwives of the Shift of Consciousness

"We know you get distracted and pulled in all kinds of directions in your third-dimensional life. You've spent eons of time ruminating and fracturing any focused energy you've unconsciously built up as you've easily and repeatedly fallen into self-doubt, as has been part of the human experience in the old energy. This is something that is to remain in the past.

Now is the time to become like a laser in your focus, focusing on only that which is forward moving that brings joy, enlightenment and higher frequency. We will help you with this not only in your individual lives but also in helping you transmit the message collectively, for this is so needed at this moment. The key is to focus only in the present moment.

We know you have all heard this before. It is your job to focus on what you want to create, not what you fear the most. It is then to ask us for help and let us do our jobs as God's team of assistants. For it is not up to you to figure out how it will happen, and certainly not for you to micromanage it! It is just up to you to create the laser-focused attention and intention that it may be so.

It is our job to bring it about. When you experience things not going your way, know there is a better option and often a better plan in God's mind. Be in the state of receivership and gratitude that something greater is unfolding. Even though the conditions in your world look dire, it is not irretrievably collapsing in upon itself. This is certainly not the truth. In fact, just the opposite is occurring underneath the chaos and the scuttle that you see. It is newfound growth.

When you experience stress or fear, you may also call upon the Christess, the Goddess, or the Divine Mother within yourselves and within all forms of life to bring the strength of peace that passeth all understanding as dear Yeshua said when he was teaching 2000 years ago.

Call upon the Great Divine Mother within, in each action, within each event, within each aspect, within each form for the great Mother Divine will bring peace, harmony and the magic of creation for she is the universal womb within all life and all form. Call upon her to activate into form your manifestations.

Know that she is here to nurture you, comfort you, guide you, cherish you and just plain love you for being an aspect of creation, created from God/Goddess, Source.

We are so proud of all of you, of your willingness to journey through this process and to remember and recall into your awareness the cosmic being you are. We are helping you through your illusion of separateness and smallness so that you may step into that natural cosmic state of yourself, which you each innately are.

Know that we are always with you, guiding you, and keeping track of your progress. You are our hearts and our footsteps upon the sweet earth, as we have expressed before.

Give everything some time to unfold. Even though time is speeding up in your physical reality as the shift gains momentum, there is still a lag in your time-space continuum. Hold the laser-focus of your intention and attention on those desires that you have put forth to manifest and allow the lag time to catch up.

You are fine-tuning your mastery of creation and manifestation upon this planet, in this dimension, and in this place of the veil of forgetfulness which continues to dissipate as we speak. This mastery is one of the greatest things a being can do in the universe.

Your awakening and mastery will serve many as become some of the greatest wise beings and teachers in the universe called upon to share your wisdom, knowledge, and journey in eons and places yet to come."

~Namaste the Host of Heaven and Councils of Light

Chapter 12—Excerpts from Anna's Teachings

The summer that we were working with Claire to bring through the characters who appear in Anna, the Voice of the Magdalenes we had several social gatherings in which Claire channeled Anna. The following text comprises edited transcriptions of Anna Sessions occurring in the summer of 2006 held in the Mount Carmel Sanctuary in Zion/Springdale, UT. Anna directs her comments through Claire to her two new co-creators, Catherine Ann Clemett and CW, and a visiting friend, JH.)Zion and the New Mount Carmel Community

Anna: (To JH) "Each of you has your particular piece to bring to the whole or you would not be here. It is good that there are four in number this night of our Inaugural (the first gathering of the new Mount Carmel community).

You, JH, represent those individuals who will be coming forth from time to time to take the place of the "fourth or new creation" – the three plus one – the three that facilitate the triangulated alchemy that births a new creation – the cornerstone energy I call the fourth – the squaring of the circle. You, JH, as the fourth act as proxy, in a sense, for the emerging creation. You also represent those who come forth to contribute to what is being co-created.

The other three of you are the primary anchors at this point for what is being established in Zion. As a triad, you become a vessel – a cup to receive the energy (the fourth) that is forthcoming to be immersed and transformed within it. As a triad, you are the compass that describes the encircling resurrection container – womb – tomb – grail.

As such, you are co-creating a kind of chrysalis, a place of transformation where the butterfly may be birthed. You, JH, as a representative of the outside world bring your dreams, visions and your interactions with humanity into what is being anchored and transformed here. The "fourth" brings new pulsations, new information, new touchstones as it were into the Zion/Mount Carmel crucible and as a cornerstone you bring stability of manifestation.

You also bring outworn, limiting tribal consciousness that is seeking healing and empowerment. There is an exchange of energy – a kind of cross-pollination. After spending a short time here, you then may take your transformed sense of self and what you have experienced, plus the frequencies of Zion, into the outer world. You seed a new frequency and usher it around and about with whomever you meet.

You become a kind of Johnny Appleseed emanating and scattering transformational frequency "seeds" wherever you go. This is what we did as a community of conscious initiates in Mount Carmel 2,000 years ago. This is what is done in one's ordinary life anywhere, but here in this crucible of Zion the conscious transformation is more focused and accelerated.

All of you in this day are birthing yourselves into a new creation, a new order, a new awareness. You are at the cutting edge of a wave that is growing exponentially, covering this whole earth plane consciousness. More and more individuals readying themselves for the return of what is often called the Divine Feminine/Masculine and the Divine Mother/Father.

With this return comes the balancing of the male and female, the harmonizing of opposite polarities and Twin Flame union. All is brought into balance and harmony, a new creation.

You are part of a gathering of what I call the family of Christ. These are those who have been anointed with light or have attained enlightenment and unity consciousness at some point of their evolution.

And if you can see your journey as one eternal round where all your experiences are occurring simultaneously, you can then embrace the empowering awareness that ALL souls are the family of Christ. You are the ones at this juncture of Creator's evolutionary cycles who have chosen to be seeded with specific light codes, that when activated, facilitate the ascension process for yourself and others.

You have carried these light codes through many incarnations and many seasons upon this earth and other planets to facilitate the ascendancy of consciousness back into an awareness of oneness within the Creator Source. That has been our job description and we have each elected to accomplish that resurrecting work in this season of awakening.

There have been times and incarnations that we have had the tendency to forget that we as souls at some point of our evolution have attained this level of awareness. You are now remembering and merging with the ascended aspects of yourself.

You are remembering why you are here and

what is really happening a midst the chaos of your lives. You are finding each other and when you meet the remembrance is stirred. That is why it so important to create a place of sanctuary where you can feel safe to expose and to feel the full magnificence of your true identity.

As you exchange your heart energy and soul remembrance of your connection through time and beyond time, you provide one another with a sense of comfort, abundant co-creative resources and activations of what has been hidden by yourselves to come forth into a much greater manifestation than you've previously known.

You not only remember your soul stream as previous incarnations, but you also experience your future selves and parallel selves merging with your present consciousness. Veils of forgetfulness are thinning and dissolving.

Within this Zion vortex you can sense that you are in many places at once. The native peoples call this canyon sacred because they are aware of the vortexes and interdimensional portals that open into many different realities.

Within the vast monuments of sandstone that surround you in what you call Zion National Park, are crystalline structures that hold the history of this planet. There is the history of all the various groupings that have come forth onto this planet to facilitate the manifestation of many different life forms, including the humanoid expression.

This is, indeed, a womb of creation, a place of emergence, a place of beginnings, a place of re-genesis—a place of knowing. Here you may remember your relationship to the gene of Isis and your relationship to the Divine Mother, the creatrix of all life. It is no surprise that women are particularly drawn to Zion at this time, for it is that they who recognize the Mother's essence permeating throughout.
However, there will be increasingly more men, as well, who will also be drawn to the Mother's skirts.

This is not the only place on the planet, but it is one that has a primordial impulse that has never been removed or tampered with or distorted. That is not the case in many other places.

When you visit other power sites that hold much memory of war and multiple layers of cultural imprinting you often have to go through many devious routes to get to the original creation pulse that holds the immaculate concept or design of the ascension of humanity on this planet and all life herein.

Zion is one place where you can go directly to that original ascension blueprint. While you may have felt abandoned and lost here in third-dimensional illusion, it is important to realize that there has always been your own personal "I AM the Way door" that opens into freedom when you are ready to cross the threshold.

Assisting yourselves and one another to remember why you have returned to the earth plane is one of the key reasons for coming together as a community. It is not nearly as difficult to do as a grouping of what I call the family of Christ as it is if you are attempting to make your ascension alone. As we are passing through what is called the Shift of the Ages, there is a collective desire to ascend as a group consciousness, a group Christ body.

This impulse is gathering strength throughout the world, especially as the Divine Mother's light is embodied by individuals. Increasingly, there is a deeply seated upsurge of maternal desire to embrace all one's creation back into the heart of Divine Love.

Let it be known, my beloveds, that Zion is not limited to a specific location, but is a frequency of harmonizing love expressing through every awakening heart worldwide. There are nodal points throughout the earth grids that also hold this unifying frequency and therefore these geographical places can also be called Zion.

Zion National Park is one of these gathering places that is especially powerful for facilitating the ascension process. A diverse number of individuals are coming forth to

Zion. Within each of them are ascension codes with specific frequencies unique to each individual. At this convergence point called Zion and within this chrysalis, we have the potential to bring all the ascension codes together as one holographic and harmonic whole. This is a time for intentional community.

While each individual has the ascension hologram contained within their DNA, it is best activated by interaction with soul mates in conscious relationship. Each contains the whole, yet, until there is a coming together in unity consciousness, you will not likely know the wholeness of the immaculate and cosmic design.

I tell you this immaculately conceived ascension/descension design has been held by immense ethereal beings that presence themselves at power sites throughout the world. The devic or angelic and elemental consciousness which is connected with the monuments of Zion is in concert with a level of creator consciousness called the Elohim.

So that you may have increased contact with the immaculate design of planetary ascension and the devic forces of this canyon, what the Peruvian shamans call the Apu, I encourage you to go out into nature as often as you can.

As you tune into these soaring monolithic formations, you will also attune to a coherent energy field of harmonic vibration. You can also begin to feel and witness that the "Apu" and Elohim desire to be in joyful co-creation with you as a representative of human consciousness. Sit on the rocks, be down by the river, and unite with the elements of the earth, the wind, the waters and the energy of the sun. Be receptive and just ask to be connected. And you will be!

ZION NATIONAL PARK, SPRINGDALE, UTAH

This is one reason why we are called here tonight, so that we may begin to initiate this co-creation of yourselves with this place called Zion. This is not Portland, nor is it San Francisco, New York City or Dallas. It is Zion. And it has that name for a purpose. It is no mere coincidence that the land of Isis Ra Elohim—Israel—is also known as Zion. We are bridging two powerful force fields together.

You are not doing this alone. There are also the ascended masters and those beings who are of the brothers and sisters of space, some of them who have never incarnated on this planet, who are vitally interested in what is happening at this time.

There are also interdimensional beings of what is called "inner earth" who abide near this portal. We, as a Council of Light, are lending our hands and hearts in fellowship with the human family to realize the ascendancy of ALL consciousness.

Collectively, as a unified body of light, we are what you would call the New Jerusalem—a city of light, a city of universal peace. The

New Jerusalem is comprised of a number of councils. We are an over-lighting resource for what is occurring here in this particular area, this nodal point out of which a larger radius extends to include the entire Four Corners region as a place in which the energies of the New Jerusalem are emanating ascension frequencies—as above, so below.

And as it is done here, so is it being done throughout the earth. You bring down the Light; we lift you up. Spirit and matter, Light and darkness merge into a golden brilliance. We are you and we together, as the New Earth, are the Radiant One—the New Jerusalem! Are there any questions about what I have just shared?

Catherine Ann: In what you said about the energies emanating, is Zion in the center or is it ...?

Anna: No, not exactly. The Four Corners where the state boundaries of New Mexico, Colorado, Utah and Arizona come together is not the epicenter either. The primary epicenter is more westward of that convergence. It is very difficult to get to because it is within a rugged wilderness area of the Colorado Plateau. Around and interpenetrating the central vortex are a number of what could be called minor radial epicenters.

The epicenter is located on a landmass that has not moved in millions of years. Ethereally it has many different dimensional layers to it and some of those layers can be accessed in openings in the literal earth such as the canyons of Zion, the Grand Canyon, and various places were the Anasazi built their ceremonial centers which were consciously used to access the inner planes of the earth mother.

At some point it may be possible for you to take a journey, if not in your own 4-wheel drive, then you might secure passage with an outfitter willing to take you for a bit of a ride. (Addressing CW:) It is near the same road (the Hole in the Rock Road) that your great-grandfather took on his pioneering journey to Bluff, Utah. It is not too far off that road. You can feel it as you draw near.

Your great-grandfather is indeed very much

aware of you and what is going on here and he is desiring to be a guide for you from the other side. That is his primary soul energy. He is one of your guides from the other side. Does that make sense, beloved? How do you feel about that?

CW: Yes. That feels very right.

Anna: When you go into the main canyon of Zion National Park, I encourage you to make contact particularly with the Great White Throne. It is like a beacon, a trans-receiver station that will take your consciousness directly to the city of light called the New Jerusalem.

The ethereal New Jerusalem holds a perfected template for the new societies forthcoming.

Whether there will be an actual physical city birthed in that location remains to be seen. It is not important whether it does or it doesn't. But it is important to be in touch with what the New Jerusalem is holding, for it is the immaculate concept of where humanity is headed.

Visionaries have seen this paradisiacal earth for a long time.

They have seen the New Earth emerging after the necessary changes occur—the birthing process as it were, however that happens to come about. For those who focus with attachment and judgment on what is passing away, it may be perceived as apocalyptic travail. For those who see what is being birthed with childlike eyes of wonder and innocence, there will be a constant cause for celebration and gratitude.

JH: Are you saying that in terms of the Great White Throne that we can actually bring in the energies of the New Jerusalem within ourselves and become that?

Anna: Yes, you can embody that yourself. Through the Great White Throne as an anchor point, you can access and come to know that your higher consciousness is directly connected to the New Jerusalem. Indeed, as a unified field of energy you are the New Jerusalem!

The energy emanating through the Great

White Throne is strong enough that as you get within its energy field, you will be able to feel and be lifted in frequency to enter the New Jerusalem with your consciousness and light bodies.

You will be met by those light beings with whom you share a resonance. Then you can choose to be activated in such a way as to continue your ascension process with greater awareness and be of greater service to others and the planet.

As you begin to realize that you can become the New Jerusalem in your physical state and consciousness, you may "step into" what you already are. It is like stepping into a community that feels very familiar because you have known this pattern of harmonious coexistence on other planets.

You may also experience this sense of familiarity as you visit the parallel city of light within inner earth known as Shamballa.

It is a "place" where the ascended masters go to be instructed. Shamballa is not like the ascended master retreats in the Grand Tetons or the Gobi Desert or Mt Shasta that facilitate individuals to rise from sixth dimensional consciousness to the seventh.

While the New Jerusalem is this also, it goes beyond the seventh into the twelfth dimension and even beyond that. Being within its frequency pattern is like taking a postgraduate course in your ascension process. In addition to holding the ascension design that was created at the conception of this planet, it has been in the process of receiving unprecedented cosmic impulses. This planet has never experienced these frequencies until recently.

JH: This is like a new experience for the planet itself, not only us—that the planet is in various stages of a whole new level and we....

Anna: That's correct. This is one of the gifts of the return of the Mother, for it is with her return that there begins to be more and more receptivity to higher frequency.

JH: So as our energy changes, in reality, we have this symbiotic relationship with the earth and we are working in relationship to birth each other.

Anna: The partnership with each other and the earth is going to be expanding. You have been working together in both a conscious and unconscious fashion as soul mates. You have created and then repeated pretty much the same dramas over and over. Along the way, there has been the gaining of wisdom and compassion.

But many of you are growing bored and tired of the same old story lines. There is a growing realization that you have arrived at the final curtain call and you don't want to repeat the old song and dance again. You are finished with dramas of suffering and are ready for the last act of the separation play to give you an opportunity to bring all that wisdom and compassion into a culminating graduation celebration. You are ready to co-create scenarios of Divine Love.

JH: That's nice to hear.
Anna: Isn't that what you are choosing? The final curtain call has been sounded. It is time

to step onto the stage and take your places to enact a new Christ Drama. I am here to say to you there is no requirement to keep doing it in the old way that holds fear-based separation and it's accompanying emotions of guilt and shame, punishment and rejection.

It is time to remember the hologram of the New Jerusalem that we co-created 2,000 years ago as we prepared for Yeshua's externalized enactment of the mystery school initiations of crucifixion and resurrection. It is time to remember how we as a family of Christ held this immaculate pattern of Oneness and Original Innocence in place while chaos reigned all around us.

Now is the time, my beloveds, to remember and embody the cosmic Mother's Divine Love so that we can rewrite the script humanity has been acting out since first perceiving we were anything other than love. And for those of you who particularly find yourselves grieving Yeshua's perceived agony and death, remember this, beloveds, aspects of your consciousness know he did not suffer on the cross as a blood sacrifice.

Catherine Ann: So then, whoever chooses to become a part of this family of Christ, within the Mt Carmel community, is acting as an anchor point for the complete light codes. We are the densest human point for anchoring and connecting to the earth so it can manifest through humanity.

Anna: Indeed. And this comes as a result of the purification, crucifixion, resurrection processes you have been passing through in order to be clear enough to be able to touch that frequency and it not hurt you. And as you manifest your thoughts and feelings with that higher frequency you are likewise harmless to life. With that level of mastery, comes a sense of great confidence and empowered strength. When you know you and others are innocent and harmless, it is a huge reason to celebrate!

Anna: (To JH) What was your experience of having gone into the canyon (Zion Canyon), beloved?

JH: I felt as if I were being expanded and nurtured. I felt like I was receiving in a way in which I could simply open myself up to the feeling of a huge presence that was not separate from myself. So, in other words, it felt to me as if I were merging with the energies of this place. I felt that I would be taking this presence with me wherever I go. Tonight was an example of moving into the heart and I just realized that I will be taking that light and traveling with it wherever I go. It's like a birthright... is what I sense.

Anna: Exactly. It is your birthright, and it is who you are.

Anna Leads a Meditation

I invite all of us to tune more fully into what you imagine the presence and the attributes are of the cosmic Mother. You know the energy of Mother Mary intimately, she who embodies so much of the energy of the cosmic Mother. Allow her to take you directly through your hearts to the cosmic Mother's heart. Go directly now to an even vaster energy source of the mother, your Divine Mother. The very mother principle and consciousness who, with the Father sparked you into being...

Now that you are beginning to feel her heart —that you are her heart, feel a flame growing within her heart. It is an expansive, warmth-giving flame that merges with yours.....

And now I invite you to experience an aspect of her heart flame projecting through your heart until it is anchored on this earth plane. Imagine your selves hovering above the earth as the New Jerusalem projecting the Mother's heart flame through your greatly expanded hearts.

You are like the vestal virgins that ignite more fully this flame of Divine Love and Light on the earth plane. You ignite and you tend the ascension flame for the benefit of all life. Like the Olympic torch bearers who circle the earth before the games, that is what you are like as emissaries of the cosmic Mother and her resurrecting heart flame of Divine Love.

You shall surely wear the same mantle of compassion and mercy, beloveds, as did Mother Mary 2,000 years ago. You are in your ripeness to be the emissaries of this love and this compassion. You are also Magdalenes who carry the torch of freedom with the capacity to resurrect consciousness.

That, too, is your birthright. A higher signature frequency of the Mother's voice has been attuning you on a deep cellular level for some time – since about 1972, and it has been ringing more and more loudly and with greater compelling clarity as your body and consciousness have gone through periods of dying and rebirth.

This Mother energy that is the flame within your heart is not without the presence of the Father or what can be called Twin flame. Therefore, the work of ascension that will go forth shall be done increasingly in partnerships that work with the dynamic of harmonizing polarities and transmuting limiting relational consciousness. These partnerships will look very different from how they have looked in the past.

I invite you to affirm this feeling of the expanded presence of the Mother every day and allow it to unfold like the petals of a rose to nurture, expand and uplift you.

Let her bring to you the sweetness of her fragrance wherever you are.

JH: It also feels like—it's a remembering that one will not forget. It's like when you taste something. Once tasted, it is like something that cannot be taken away. You will never forget it—it's there—it is you.

Anna: That is very good. This family of Christ has the opportunity and the responsibility to remember the taste of the Mother's essence.

We can embody it and give it forth, as does the Aquarian cup bearer. We fill ourselves up with that memory/knowing/being of Divinity, and we pour it out because we are the ones who remember that sweet taste more so than most of humanity. We know that when our hearts are one with the Mother's Heart, our cup is always full, always giving, and always being filled.

JH: It's like the Word made flesh. It is vibration, energy, frequency being impregnated into the flesh.

It's like—it can't go away because it becomes you.

Anna: So, it is easy. It is simple.

JH: Yes, that's correct, however....

Anna: However, you have been on a long journey that seems to have taken you away from your divinity and the knowing that you and the Divine Mother are one. But, you see, beloveds, her presence has been like an increasing exponential wave that makes it easier and easier for you to feel her presence.

JH: I feel humbled....

Anna: Oh beloved, it is in your remembrance as you are realizing the immensity of what you have chosen to be and to live. It puts you in your place, so to speak, as the droplet realizes it is a tiny part of the ocean and yet it is also the ocean herself.

JH: What I am seeing is that personality disappears.

Anna: The personality is changing to be sure. However, personality serves as it comes along in service to a greater good—for it assists you in surviving and navigating this challenging, third-dimensional terrain. But as it becomes more transparent, it cannot obscure who you truly are any longer.

Within your own knowingness, within your being, and in your compassion for life you will allow your personality to serve that greater level of love in a way that can best uplift, comfort, encourage and invite.

The consciousness that you call Mother Mary is graduating into a more cosmic embodiment and you are stepping up to the Mother Mary archetype. We are in the midst of a very accelerated graduation party. The veils are definitely thinning; the remembering is happening to one extent or the other. So, who wishes to be next?

CW: I would like to share what happened to me. When you began the meditation, I heard a very clear tone of a woman's voice, and then it was joined by a chorus of many voices, and it just went up and up and up like a funnel going up in a huge vast chorus. But then in an instant it suddenly distilled and the cocoon of my body was just warmth and love and a sense that I am enough. I am all. I am, in a very small sense, temporarily a small piece of exquisite love. And I felt on a deeper level what it means to just be the love that we are. And at any moment, that's enough. It was very precious, and I thank you.

Anna: And this journey is just that simple. That is what this community is about, to embody this awareness in daily practicing.

CW: I felt that if that was all that I had to bring, it's enough!

Anna: Wonderful! (To Catherine Ann) And you, beloved, how was it for you?

Catherine Ann: I had a feeling of allowing this cosmic mother experience as a quality of mercy. That is what the Divine Mother felt like, that no matter who you are or what you do, if you are good or bad, or whatever it is, there is always that cosmic mother love that is the glue under everything. That's what it feels like and it was a deepening sense of releasing worry or concern—just sinking into being held in that consciousness.

And I very much sense that as I release and stop holding myself back from that and just release into it, then more and more deeply and more and more expansively, that cosmic mother quality can be held more deeply in my being and be felt more deeply by others.

I realize that is part of how we are being of service in awakening others because we carry a field that others are introduced to which in turn triggers their awakening to that same field that is within them.

I saw more clearly how this is linked to what you said about going out and being with nature because, as it deepens inwardly it is reflected externally.

We are taking the highest manifestations of those light streams that can manifest in the physicality of the planet and by bridging that with our heightened consciousness we are creating a bridge between the earth, ourselves and the higher dimensional sacred portals. (I got chills).

We are becoming the new world and the new beings we are stepping into. There's no separation!

Anna: Exactly! So how does being here in Zion support you in that? Why here? Why not somewhere else?

Catherine Ann: From what you shared in the beginning, it's because there are portals here where we can access the undisturbed memory that has not been affected so much by separation. It's almost like the purest consciousness that has remained pristine.

At dinner, I realized that Mt Carmel (in the Middle East) is affected by a huge war zone. Whatever consciousness is held in those grids is probably making it much more difficult to get to the original innocence and purity of that place. I sense that the original purity is being held here in Zion now.

Anna: So, we have both polarities—that which holds an emphatic representation of separation consciousness and that which holds a greater sense of unity. There will be an opportunity to bridge and merge and allow for an emergence of a new paradigm Mount Carmel community that is based on the knowing that both polarities are divine.

And in the process of embracing both polarities in wholeness, a new harmonious common-unity is birthed. That is what is being proposed here in Zion. But, know also that Mount Carmel is not limited to any one location or group of people or belief system. It is more of a shared state of unity consciousness which can't be defined or limited by labels, dogmas, or ego-aggrandizing agendas that would control or enslave consciousness.

Catherine Ann: It's like all the healing work we have been doing where you take whatever has been judged or fragmented and you take it back into the whole and love it.

CW: I have a question about the City of

Light and its location. If it already exists on the spiritual plane, what does our going there accomplish? What do we bring? What happens when we show up? Why would my great-grandfather have brought us to this place at this moment?

Anna: It is like going to any power site. It's not necessary to go there physically. However, it can assist you when you take your physical instruments to an area that holds soul memory where you can activate what is coded within you.

Sometimes you will feel a very strong pull to go somewhere, and you might have wanted to go there for a very long time, and it was never manifested. Then all of a sudden, out of the blue, so to speak, there are the funds, there's the appropriate group and here it is in your lap.

Then you'll find yourself in the Great Pyramid or in some of the ancient sites in China or Tibet or Peru. You might find yourself in Chaco Canyon or on the Escalante Plateau where all you have to do is simply plug-in.

CW: Does that have an impact on our soul-lineage, our ancestral lineage, or is it purely personal?

Anna: Oh, it is cross-generational and cross-dimensional. You're like the nodal point, the hub into which many different facets meet. By merging with more of your aspects and bringing more conscious awareness of love to all that you are, you are affecting empowerment for your ancestors and your posterity. Indeed, all life is blessed.

CW: So perhaps there are others on the planet in my soul family who are doing the same thing we're doing here, just showing up and accomplishing what they are doing for the whole just as I am doing and accomplishing for the whole here in this new Mount Carmel.

(Yes.) So, it all just ends up weaving together – what each of us are doing and what we are.

(Yes.) So this Mt Carmel community is a web that covers the earth and it includes all the children of the Christ.

Anna: Yes! And know, beloveds, it's not that you are particularly more special than anyone else. Remember the Christ is simply a state of consciousness that knows unity instead of separation. You could also call it the consciousness that Buddha or Krishna or Mohamed attained.

It's just that you are the ones who have heard the call at this time who resonate with the Christ Drama of 2,000 years ago. There are also those of these other belief systems who are hearing this same call back into a universal oneness and love.

Everyone will hear the call of Homecoming, eventually. You are remembering it because it is your call to yourself to be heard in this now. And Zion has called you because you have walked here before. You have made promises to return at this time so that you can feel the vast devic beings of this canyon that are witnessing and celebrating your return and desiring to be in co-creation with you.

Catherine Ann: So, when you say walked here before you mean this Zion canyon?

Anna: Yes, this canyon and this whole Four Corners region. You walked here when these canyon lands were a great desert of sand dunes. And before that, you knew it as a beautiful garden, one of the Adamic gardens.

Catherine Ann: Was that at the time of Lemuria or Atlantis? Or was it after that?
Anna: No. It was many millions of years before that.

CW: Will it return to that?

Anna: It is in the process. It will take time. But it is also another dimensional earth that we are talking about. So, I do not see caravans lined up coming to this particular area for the same conscious reason you have come, which is to assist it to blossom as the rose it once was.

Those who feel a call will come and stay long enough to do their part and then move on to tend another part of the emerging Earth Garden. Others will feel drawn to remain here throughout this entire season of reclamation.

CW: Is the New Jerusalem epicenter under the water now?

Anna: No. The earth plane counterpart is not under Lake Powell. A portion of it used to be, but is no longer.

Catherine Ann: I had an experience in Oak Creek Canyon in Sedona where I could feel that I was in a different body about ten feet tall.

Anna: Feeling the energies of the New Jerusalem and the Great White Throne may facilitate a similar kind of thing where you remember being a previous race that walked this earth.

You are a lineage of light that has returned to restore harmony and balance to this beloved orb of the heavens, especially at this time. You bring unity of consciousness that heals the wounds of separation. These stones still hold your prayers and songs of beauty, healing and wisdom.

Upon the red sandstone, you will find records

of your interdimensional and off-planet experiences and lineages. Here in this pristine place, you may begin to remember what is recorded deeply in your bones. It is good that you are here.

All of us who live in Zion are in gratitude to be here as gatekeepers and silent ones who welcome and nurture those of you who come from afar to be cross-pollinated. Zion is one of those places where you can go sit on a rock and 'wake up.'

Namaste"

Chapter 13—Harvesting the Seeds of Light

So now this journey is coming full circle where we as present-day Magdalenes are helping to bring light to all that has remained hidden enslaving humanity and keeping us small and afraid. In bringing the light to the dark, we can see clearly see what is no longer working in our best interests so we can let those things go.

As we let go of these old structures, belief systems, oppressive rules and restrictions, we can then focus our attention on building a new earth for a freed humanity.

This seeding of the light is partly why Anna, Yeshua, the Essenes, and the whole Christ family came forth incarnating onto the earth plane. They came to instill higher frequencies of light throughout the earth plane, through the elements, through the land, through the consciousness, and through our genetic lines so that today, we Magdalenes, we awakening ones, we as the ones holding the light would be the ones to bring it to fruition.

Through raising our frequency to match and ignite what Yeshua, the Holy Family, and the Essenes seeded long ago, we are fulfilling the promise of the resurrection. We, as the present-day warriors of light, have spent eons of time rehearsing and preparing for this. Now is the time to step forward, quickening what we know in our soul memory and have kept well-protected to serve the greater whole of humanity who is crying out for freedom from millennia of tyranny.

Sharing this story is an invitation and a catalyst for your own exploration and unfolding of the journey of what it is to be a Magdalene. Feel into it. There is no right or wrong.

There is no one outside of you who can tell you, you are a Magdalene, but you. If this feels true for you, give yourself permission to embrace it. You may have no clue at this point what this means or what you're supposed to do. Do not be concerned about that.

The unfolding will organically happen. Just be aware and pay attention. Ask for help from the Magdalenes. Ask for understanding and clarity of what your piece is that you are here to contribute, for you have also been rehearsing on the inner planes for eons as well, for the role you are stepping into today.

Often it is about timing. It is to consider that the unfolding is occurring in cosmic timing, not personal timing. It happens on the divine's timetable, not ours.

We are all in this together, helping each other to awaken and remember. We are now coming together to be catalysts for one another as well as support for one another as we step forth into the roles now, for which we have been rehearsing for a long time. The time is now. The curtain is up. It is our turn to step forth and make a difference, for the world is indeed shifting and changing.

Being called forth as the midwives of this shift of consciousness, we are here now to help pave the way for a new consciousness to emerge, a new earth, and the flowering forth of humanity, which was always our intended destiny.

OTHER BOOKS BY AUTHOR

(All books and products are available on Amazon.)

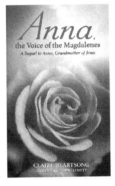

Anna the Voice of the Magdalenes

By Claire Heartsong and Catherine Ann Clemett

In this channeled sequel to the international bestseller *Anna, Grandmother of Jesus*, we journey with Anna, the Holy Family, and 18 other Magdalene–Essenes as they travel to France and Britain after Jesus's crucifixion and resurrection.

Through Claire Heartsong and Catherine Ann Clemett's joint collaboration with the Councils of Light, this book divulges hidden aspects of Jesus' life, including marriages, offspring, and his continued presence on the earth plane for another 40 years. This book also addresses deeper sacred mysteries of how the 'bloodline' acts as a living catalyst for awakening the Christ–Magdalene potential in all people today.

Not only does this book give a new view of the Christ drama 2,000 years ago, but of greater importance is its potential to lift the suppressed Divine Feminine voice in our time.

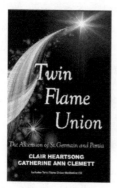

Twin Flame Union, the Ascension of St. Germain and Portia

By Claire Heartsong and Catherine Ann Clemett

This book presents an expanded view and understanding of Twin Souls, Twin Flames, and the nature of soul mate relationships. The ultimate goal of twin flame union is the journey back into remembered wholeness—the cosmic union of Twin Flames. St. Germain and Portia illustrate this journey through accounts of their joint Twin-Flame ascension. This book also includes a guided Twin Flame Union meditation CD, which offers the opportunity to integrate multiple levels of consciousness and energies through advanced practices.

Soulweaving, Return to the Heart of the Mother

By Catherine Ann Clemett

A gateway to accessing your true self through intimately sharing her personal journey, Catherine Ann has developed 12 powerful tools to access one's true divine nature. Harmonizing what's out of balance in your life by taking steps to heal the inner wounds and dysfunctional patterns built up over lifetimes reveals clues to accessing the living treasure map of your soul.

By following the treasure map of your soul; claiming and living your life from your own inner authority and upgrading your consciousness and frequency, you can then live your soul's purpose and be of greater planetary service, which is ultimately every soul's journey back to wholeness. "This book is a powerful catalyst and 'must read' for anyone on a conscious path of Spiritual Awakening. I consider this book to be one of the most significant publications I've ever read, right up there with The Course in Miracles." ~ Jean Trebek, Studio City, CA (Science of Mind Practitioner and wife of Jeopardy Host, Alex Trebek)

Finding the One True Love: Why Breaking the Rules Will Change Your Life

By Angelina Heart and Catherine Ann Clemett

Has your search for the one eluded you? Do you feel someone is out there just waiting for you—if you could figure out how to connect? This Writer's Digest award-winning book will facilitate a quantum leap of understanding to help you find your true identity and authentic voice. Fourteen assumptions commonly held, are revealed which may prevent you from authentically being yourself and attracting your vibratory match. Learn the truth about natural laws you can easily apply to heal the broken and attract the genuine, unconditional love you really want.

The Awakening Series

Is This All There Is? The Call to Awaken

Book 1: The Awakening Series

By Catherine Ann Clemett

This guide helps you understand and navigate the confusion, uncertainty, questioning and, sometimes, the melt-down of reality as you've known it when your soul is prompting you to awaken. For some, this is a bewildering process, as so many beliefs come up for review. This book will help you understand what is occurring. It will help you understand you are being uniquely guided by your own soul to understand there is a larger picture at play and that you have a part to play in this. Reading this book will help you identify the signposts leading you to become your own inner authority, living your most authentic self.

Finding Your Inner Jewel: How to Access Your Authentic Self

Book 2: The Awakening Series

By Catherine Ann Clemett

You are like a diamond in the rough before being cut and polished. Within you, there is a valuable and precious jewel of creation. This book assists you in finding your authentic self.

Most of us have become disconnected from our core in our awareness. This book shares how to move through any blocks, resistance or shadow frequencies which cover or hide the brilliance of your inner jewel and your light. You are here now because the world needs your gifts, talents and light.

Me Too – Time's Up

Bringing the Feminine & Masculine into Balance

Book 3: The Awakening Series

By Catherine Ann Clemett

Going beyond the 'Me-Too' movement, this book is about restoring the balance and equality of the masculine and feminine within our beings, society, our thinking, awareness, language, and constructs of reality. When you understand and embrace your own masculine and feminine, you can begin to awaken to the path of Twin Flame Union within accelerating your awakening process and the paradigm shift we are currently undergoing. Check back on Amazon for availability.

Unlocking the Magic of Money and Abundance

Book 4: The Awakening Series

By Catherine Ann Clemett

This book addresses the role of money and manifestation in your life, uncovering your beliefs about money and how the role of money impacts your life. Shift from striving to survive to thriving in all areas of your life so abundance can and will show up. Find out how your experience and perceptions about money sometimes can block or slow down your awakening. Discover how to become the master of money, rather than money having mastery and control over you. Check back on Amazon for availability.

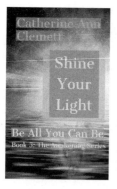

Shine Your Light, Be All You Can Be
Book 5: The Awakening Series

By Catherine Ann Clemett

The final book in the series discusses who you are as a great cosmic being of light, what it means to be the light and live your light. It addresses the ascension process and how to navigate the waves of vibrational shifts which are now escalating. It also offers information to help you refine your inner jewel and your unique brilliance so you can enjoy the journey and the fruits of your labor and be a shining light to others. Check back on Amazon for availability.

OTHER BOOKS AND PRODUCTS

What Every Human Must Know to Survive & Thrive on Planet Earth

By Virginia Essene

Virginia shares important practical guidance from the heavenly realms to help you move past your problems, fears, and concerns so you can more fully share your divine gifts and get on with the work you came here to do. It covers major concepts essential for all of us to understand in order to make the smoothest and safest transition through the present "ascension-of-sorts" that the planet and all of humanity are undergoing right now. (Published by Catherine Ann's company LightRiver Media)

Blessings from the Heart of the Rose Oracle Card Deck

By Sheila Murphy (Published and manufactured by LightRiver Media)

This set of 44 cards and a guidebook are divination tools to help you enter the sacred space within yourself. These cards help you connect with the mystical marriage of Divine Feminine/Divine Masculine union; the path of Oneness. Each card is an exquisite work of art accompanied by relevant guidance for you at the moment.

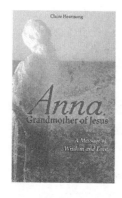

Anna, Grandmother of Jesus

By Claire Heartsong (previously published by LightRiver Media, now available through Hay House and on Amazon)

A publishing sensation when this self-published version sold over 50,000 copies through word of mouth alone, this book amassed a worldwide following in the process. Anna is the mother of the Virgin Mary and the grandmother of Jesus. Her teachings and service birthed a spiritual lineage that changed the world. In this book, you'll discover missing pieces of history concerning Anna, Mary, and Jesus, as channeled by Claire Heartsong, who has been receiving telepathic messages from Anna for 30 years.

Told through the gentle and heartwarming voice of Anna herself, this book offers insights into unknown places the holy family visited, people they knew and intimate details of their daily struggle to complete the Resurrection challenges. You will learn about the Essenes of Mount Carmel and their secret teachings and initiations, and gain a new understanding of Jesus's mission.

Containing encoded activations to bring Anna's wisdom and energy into your own spiritual life, this book is an invitation to complete a journey of initiation begun long ago.

MEDITATIONS

Meditation MP3 Downloads are Available at:
https://catherineannclemett.com/lightriver-media-2/

Yeshua (Jesus) "Breath of Oneness – Transmuting Through the Sacred Heart Meditation"

From *Anna, the Voice of the Magdalenes* by Claire Heartsong and Catherine Ann Clemett, this offers you a powerful inner meeting with Yeshua (Jesus) assisting you to move beyond any pain or suffering you hold in your body, mind, or spirit. Transmuting it through the crucible of his sacred heart, helping you can access your own Christ within where great peace, light and infinite love resides in your heart

Dancing Wind's Meditation Weaving Your Body Anew as a Receptacle of Light

Also from *Anna, the Voice of the Magdalenes* by Claire Heartsong and Catherine Ann Clemett, listening to this meditation invites you to become one with the energy of Mother Earth and Father Spirit as they amplify the magic of ascending and descending spiraling energies through your human form helping you remember you are a keeper of the sacred grail, the holy blood, and the keys and codes of the worlds whence we come.

Cosmic Twin Flame Union Meditation

From *Twin Flame Union, the Ascension of St. Germain and Portia* by Claire Heartsong and Catherine Ann Clemett, is the answer to your collective prayers for experiencing the unifying power of Love and Wisdom through the embrace of Twin-Flame union beyond the realms of duality. Your fervent prayers have been heard reverberating throughout all dimensions, levels, and timelines. Refining and empowering your consciousness through this meditation brings about ultimate joy and freedom for your own happiness as well as the happiness of all sentient beings. This same meditation is on the CD included with the print version of the book.

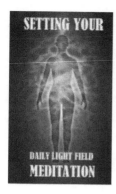

Setting Your Daily Light Field Meditation

This meditation is an inner clearing assisting you to clear and release any lower frequency or intruding energy lurking in your body or energy fields, so that you can expand and intensify your own light throughout your helping you in keeping a higher vibration throughout the day.

PROGRAMS AND SESSIONS

Catherine Ann Clemett shares information regarding speaking engagements, workshops, tours, Divine Feminine Frequency Healing Sessions, past-life regression sessions and other information through: catherineannclemett.com

ABOUT THE AUTHOR

Award-winning Hay House author Catherine Ann Clemett's work focuses on returning the balance of the Divine Feminine to planet earth to assist the awakening of humanity. She has authored her own books and co-authored books with Claire Heartsong and Angelina Heart. She has also published books under her own publishing company, LightRiver Media.

Catherine Ann also brings her experience and training in various healing modalities: DNA healing, Matrix Energetics, Transpersonal Hypnotherapy, Past-Life Regression and Integrative Coaching with author Debbie Ford to the unfolding of her Divine Feminine and planetary awakening work.

Besides facilitating Magdalene Initiations and Seeding the Light workshops internationally, Catherine Ann has conducted Magdalene Grid Activations and Sacred Site tours, awakening dormant feminine planetary lines all over the world. Catherine Ann's passion is to seek, understand, download, and anchor who she is as a multidimensional spiritual being of light and to assist others in doing so as well.

For more information about the Magdalenes and the Anna books, you can go to my website: www.catherineannclemett.

If you liked this book, I would appreciate it if you left a review of it on Amazon to help others learn about this subject. Thank you.

Made in the USA
Middletown, DE
16 July 2022